Woodbrooke College
200 28196

D1634633

THE FOUR LAST THINGS

BY

H. A. WILLIAMS

Dean of Chapel, Trinity College
Cambridge

LONDON

A. R. MOWBRAY & Co. LIMITED

To JAMES, because he has been there.

First published in 1960

PRINTED IN GREAT BRITAIN BY
A. R. MOWBRAY & CO. LIMITED IN THE CITY OF OXFORD
0176

CONTENTS

AUTHOR'S NOTE

These four talks were given on the Home Service of the B.B.C. during November and December, 1959. They are published as broadcast.

H. A. W.

THE FOUR LAST THINGS

I

DEATH

IN the four weeks before Christmas it is traditional for Christians to consider what they call the Last Things. These Last Things are death, judgement, hell, and heaven. When you think what Christmas means—peace on earth and goodwill towards men—it may seem strange that we should prepare for it by dwelling on death, judgement, and so forth. What have these Last Things to do with the Babe of Bethlehem?

But the word 'last' here doesn't refer to what comes after everything else in a time-sequence—it's not like the last train home coming after all the other trains of the day. Last means ultimate or fundamental. For example, I quarrel with John Smith about this, that, and the other. He was curt with me this morning. This afternoon he played his wireless too loud. The smoke from his bonfire came into my garden. But my real, fundamental quarrel with him is that he has got the job that I wanted. His job—that is my last quarrel with John Smith. In the same way, the so-called Last Things relate to what human life is really about, fundamentally about. Superficially, our life seems a chance collection of circumstances, a random succession of pleasure and pain. But in Christ, God became man in order to break through this superficial surface, in order to put human life in its true context, in order to show that ultimate issues are being decided in what often feels like the whirligig of our existence. That is what death, judgement, hell, and heaven have to do with Christmas. The Man born at Bethlehem, in all He did and suffered, showed us that every day we live we are confronted with them: that they are not merely something which happens to us after we have drawn our final breath: that they are with us here and now.

How are they with us? In what sense are we dying and dead? How can we recognize that last trump which all the time is sounding to summon us before the judgement-seat of Christ? When are we in heaven and when are we in hell? Now, don't misunderstand me. Christians down the ages have used these terms to speak of man's condition after he has left this world by means of physical death. I am not denying that they can and ought to be used in this way. What I want to suggest is that these terms won't tell us anything about what we call the future life unless we have learned to recognize them in this life. The New Testament is founded upon the paradox that in the coming of Christ the future did not remain simply future, but also became part of the present. So, for instance, Jesus said, 'Now is the judgement of this world'; while St. Paul reminds the Philippians, almost as a commonplace, 'Our citizenship is (now) in heaven.' In these broadcasts, therefore, we shall try to discover how the Last Things impinge upon us in the present. To-night I shall speak of death. On the three following Thursdays, of judgement, hell, and heaven.

Almost everybody is instinctively afraid of dying. Why? I don't think it is the fear of punishment. I know that what we do has moral consequences which may be profoundly disturbing. But in themselves, these consequences don't make dying any more frightening than living. After all, our life now is full of reaping what we have sown. Our past actions meet us every day. Is then the fear of death the fear of extinction? Certainly it isn't. Have you ever tried to make your flesh creep by imagining you had never been born? You can't do it. If you had never been born, there wouldn't be any you there to mind. Extinction would be exactly identical. There couldn't be anything to worry about if there wasn't anybody to be worried. What, then, makes people afraid of dying? It's the fear of losing control over ourselves. True, our control is never complete. All the time we are being pushed about by circumstances beyond our control. Yet within these limits we still exercise a certain sovereignty. Until the ship founders we are still its masters, however strong the winds or rough the sea. Our hand is still on the wheel. Death means our hand dropping away, our no longer being able to steer. We are abandoned to the elements and they must take us where they will. This is the true terror of death.

But this fear of losing control over ourselves is one which is always with us, at least below the surface. You meet it, for instance, when you go into a house where everything is always exactly in its place. The householder can't rest if a single book is not in its proper position on the right shelf. He is thus trying to cope with the fear of losing control, the fear of death, though he probably doesn't know it. Or consider how people grasp at power. On a big scale a Hitler wants to dominate the world. He says it is the mission of Germany to do so. On a small scale, I want to dominate my children, or my friends. I say it's because I know best. Behind the reasons given lies a strategy of defence. My control over others makes me feel more secure against the threatened loss of all control. It is the fear of death which is forcing me on. Or consider once again how fanatically we often cling to the past, refusing to recognize that it is dead. I'm an old man, but on Christmas morning I still go bathing in the Serpentine. It was once a tremendous thrill. Now it is agonizing and always gives me a cold which will one day turn to pneumonia. I clutch at the thrill even though it isn't there and can't ever be there again. We all do that in some way or other. When they married, John and Mary were ecstatically in love. That was ten years ago. By now, the ecstasy should have been replaced by something else; a close companionship, enriching, creative, satisfying but different. Yet they cling to the ecstasy even though it isn't there, and in the nature of the case can't be there. They blame each other for its absence, and are miserable. In fact their misery is due to their fear of dying—of dying to what they once were. So they cling to a dead past. We sometimes complain of people that they are behaving childishly. A careful analysis of human behaviour shows that most people are in some particular out of date in their reactions to circumstances. A colleague tells me that my talks are hopelessly bad. This criticism is felt by me as a most terrible disaster. It makes me feel that it's hardly worth going on living. I am thoroughly upset. Why is my reaction to this criticism so extreme? Because in my feelings here I am still a small child. My colleague has turned into a parent upon whom as a small child I depend for everything absolutely. Since this parent has turned against me, I am indeed lost. Hence the strength of my feelings. They arise from my not having yet died to my infancy.

There is something in common between these illustrations. In each case I cling on to whatever it is, because I feel that, if I don't, there will be nothing left. I must therefore clutch at some caricature of order. I must clutch at some unsatisfying sense of power. I must clutch at what I was, even sometimes my very infancy. For if I don't, I shall be annihilated. I shall die.

Jesus spoke quite often about this. He emphasized that death is one of the fundamental facts of human life; so if you had asked Him what human life is really about, He would have answered, 'It's about dying.' And He would have gone on to say, 'It's only by being ready to die that you will be able to live.' Those, of course, are my words. Listen to His: 'Whosoever seeks to gain his life will lose it, but whosoever loses his life will preserve it.' 'Unless a grain of wheat falls into the earth and dies, it remains alone, but if it dies, it bears much fruit. He who loves his life loses it, and he who hates his life in this world will keep it for eternal life.' Jesus saw that all the time men and women are being faced with the challenge of death; and that if they are to grow into full maturity, they must not clutch at this or that aspect of themselves. They must take the risk, the awful risk, of letting it go. They must, in other words, be ready to die daily. For this was the path, the only path, to complete life. What Jesus preached, He also practised. He allowed everything to be stripped away from Him, and died naked upon a cross. So He passed through the grave and gate of death to His joyful resurrection. 'I am He that liveth and was dead; and behold, I am alive for evermore.'

This is the Gospel. Christ's resurrection assures us that the loss of which we are so frightened, real though it is, is not final. We surrender, we give up, only in order to receive what is better. So Jesus surrendered His human life. And God gave it back to Him, now infinitely more than human. 'Whosoever would save his life,' said Jesus, 'will lose it; and whosoever loses his life for My sake and the gospel's will save it.'

We can't make ourselves die. We can leave our books lying about the room in untidy heaps; we can bite our lips and prevent ourselves bossing other people about; we can give up our bathe on Christmas Day; John can say to himself over and over again, 'I'm no longer looking to Mary for the past, but for something else, something new'; and I can behave as though I minded only a little when my colleague tells me how bad my talks are. But what's the use of this outward pantomime when all the time I'm exactly the same inside? After all, the inside, that's the real me. We can't make ourselves die. But Jesus spoke of losing our life 'for My sake and the gospel's.' It's not a matter of trying but of trusting. Trust God to bring home to you the truth of His Gospel in Christ, so that slowly it sinks to the very depths of your being, and becomes no longer just a message but a real part of you. To the degree in which this happens you will find yourself dying—and living. And when in due course the time comes for you to draw your final breath, you will no longer be frightened. The surrender then required of you will be something of which you already have experience. You will know death as the harbinger of life.

II

JUDGEMENT

IN these talks during Advent we are considering what Christians call the Last Things, and how they impinge upon us in the present. Last week I spoke of death. To-day I am going to speak about judgement.

When we think of judgement we think of a law-court and of a judge passing sentence upon the convicted criminal. This was the picture with which St. Paul started out when he was writing to the Christians in Rome about God's dealings with men. Man was in the dock and God was the judge. But as Paul amplified his theme, the law-court he described became a very odd affair indeed. There was no need for a prosecutor since the accused pleaded guilty. Well, that sometimes happens. The bizarre nature of the proceedings, however, began to be shown in the reasons which led the accused to plead guilty. These were the obvious desire of the judge to become the intimate friend of the criminal. In fact, so concerned was the judge for the criminal's well-being that you could see he was suffering acutely on his account. And it was the sight of the judge's suffering which led the criminal to confess. The confession made, the judge proceeded to acquit him. And in the acquittal of this guilty man, Paul comments, we see justice in its highest form. For the judge was looking, not at the man as he was, but at the man as he could and would become as a result of the judge's close friendship.

Well, that's Paul's picture of God's judgement-seat. You will see that it certainly isn't a picture of a law-court as we understand it. Nor is it a case simply of judgement being tempered by mercy. The mercy is primary all the way along—the judge's suffering concern for the criminal. It is in the context of this mercy that the criminal is led to judge himself, to admit his fault. And this admission makes it possible for judgement to be pronounced in his favour. The result is that he begins to become a new man.

What St. Paul here sets before us in a picture we can see happening as a matter of history to the first disciples of Jesus. It is the night before He died, and He is having His last meal with them in the Upper Room. The disciples are quarrelling among themselves—which of them is the most important? Jesus points out to them that from the human point of view the man sitting at dinner is more important than the servant who waits. Yet He, their Master, is among them as he that serveth. Jesus then goes to the cross, and shows how He serves His disciples to His last breath. He serves them by suffering for them and giving them all He has got. The vision of this suffering love is for the disciples the day of judgement. Looking at the Crucified, they see how mean and squalid are their petty squabbles and self-importance. In the light of Christ's love, they pass judgement upon themselves. And this judgement is a new beginning. It initiates a life of surrender to the love which serves, enabling them to convert the world.

Notice here that the effect of standing before the judgement-seat of Christ is never simply negative. It doesn't stop at condemnation. If we are led to condemn ourselves, that is because we have become aware of the glorious destiny God has prepared for us. We are to be His friends, fellow-workers with Christ in renewing the world by the fire of His love. What we have been in the past is condemned only in view of what we can be and will be in the future. 'For God sent not His Son into the world to condemn the world; but that the world through Him might be saved.' And Jesus Christ is the same yesterday, to-day, and for ever. It is necessary to emphasize this point. First because, although we must use the analogy of the human judge, it can be fundamentally misleading. And secondly, much more important, imperfect as we still are, there is in most of us a residuum of hatred of which we are scarcely aware. This hatred is that part of our power to love which has gone sour. Until we are perfect we cannot fully mobilize all our potential for loving. And the love thus unused turns to hatred. On the whole, we generally know when we are directing our hatred at other people. It is less easy for us to see what we are doing when we are directing this hatred at ourselves. If we are Christians, one of the ways in which we may direct such hatred at ourselves is to paint a picture of Jesus Christ as a ruthless, avenging judge bent on condemning us for good and all. There is no creative quality about the judgement of this false constructed Christ. The sentence which this Christ passes is a dead-end. So let us not confuse *him* with the Crucified. He is not the Son of God's love: he is the product of my own diseased imagination—a self-portrait of that part of me of which I am not directly aware, myself as hating—whose nature it is to kill and to destroy. Satan, said Jesus, cannot cast out Satan. My hatred, even when, especially when, it is my hatred of me, can never serve the purposes of love. When I condemn myself at Christ's judgement-seat it is never because I hate. It is because I have fallen in love with what God can make of me. There is all the difference in the world between those two attitudes, though in practice they are often terribly confused. This is what has made a great deal of Christian exhortation on the theme of judgement so profoundly un-Christian. As of old, it is Satan masquerading as an angel of light; it is my denial of love, unknown even to myself, piously disguised as a messenger of Christ.

So let us always remember that Christ the judge is none other than Jesus of Nazareth who brought His disciples to judgement by dying for them.

But for Christians, Jesus Christ is not only an historical figure of the past. He is the creator of the universe who holds in His hands all things that exist. In St. John's well-known words: 'All things were made through Him, and without Him was not anything made that was made.' Just, therefore, as we find the character of the artist in the pictures he paints, so we shall expect to find the Christ shown forth to us in the world He has made. We do not yet see Him face to face. We see Him as He is reflected in His workmanship. In other words, we may see Him in all that is, in the whole manifold variety of our human experience. There is no corner of life where we may not find ourselves confronted with Him. For in Him all things hold together. This means that the day of judgement is always to-day. It is not something to wait for in some indefinite future.

Christ is with us now in the world He made. Our judge is here in all the circumstances of our lives. He makes Himself known to people in a countless variety of ways. The examples I am about to suggest almost certainly won't be the way He will appear as *your* judge. But I offer them in the hope that they may perhaps help you to keep your eyes open for Him.

Suppose, for instance (may I repeat that this probably won't happen to you?), but suppose the plight of the millions of refugees in the world is suddenly brought home to me—their suffering, their hopelessness, their desperate need of love and care. As it happens I have no ties. I am free to do what I like. Up till now, I have given a reasonable amount of time to voluntary work. But, like most other people, I have also kept quite a lot of time for the pursuit of my own pleasure. But now I feel an overwhelming call to give myself entirely to the displaced persons in refugee camps. I don't feel at all conceited as a result of my decision. Indeed, it seems to have been made for me when the need of these people was borne in upon my consciousness and I realized I was free to go. But I am deeply aware of, and profoundly thankful for, the ineffable splendour of my new calling. It's odd that it should have come to me. I'm such a selfish person really and have always been frightfully concerned about my own comfort. I didn't realize how shabby my life was until now, when I'm going to leave it.

This person in our story has stood before the judgement-seat of Christ. Perhaps we are being too dramatic—though such things do happen. So let us take the more ordinary case of Smith, who has been a good father in a way, but has never really tried to understand his children. Now that they are growing up it makes things rather difficult. They need a father's advice, and this is just what he can't give them. Mercifully for all concerned, Smith, who has always been a loyal husband, now falls in love with the typist at the office who doesn't return his feelings the least bit. He can't understand what's come over him. He's always been a sane, level-headed chap, who has loudly condemned every sort of nonsense in his children. But now he sees that life isn't so obvious as he thought. The agony caused him by the attractive Miss Jones at the office leads him to think he could have been a very much better father to Tom when he was madly in love with that usherette. Understanding, that's what people wanted—even middle-aged people like him, let alone the young. He'd been an unhelpful brute. But now Miss Jones had taught him better. Our Mr. Smith has stood before the judgement-seat of Christ.

Forgive one final example. Suppose I say my prayers and go to church regularly and keep the commandments. I call myself a Christian and I argue for the truth of Christianity with the agnostic next door. Up the road there is a blind man on whom I'd always meant to call and never did. When the blind man dies, I discover that my agnostic friend has been reading to him three times a week. There, I think, is real love, and it makes all my arguing for Christianity look very flat indeed. I know now what I've been searching for—the spirit of Christ which, for all my clever words, was never mine.

Human life is fundamentally concerned with this fact

of judgement. Time and time again circumstances demand of us a reappraisal of ourselves and our manner of life. And this reappraisal, Christians believe, can be true and trustworthy only if it comes as the result of a new vision of future possibilities. It is the person that God is slowly making me into which reappraises the person I have been. It is my future in God's Providence which judges my past, my destiny which judges my history. Here and now we can only dimly guess at what God has in store for us. As St. Paul said: 'Eye hath not seen, nor ear heard, neither have entered into the heart of man the things which God hath prepared for them that love Him.' The more we know of such things, the more radical will be our revaluation of ourselves. The final judgement is thus the vision of God, when we see Him as He is.

III

HELL

THIS evening I'm to speak about hell. Perhaps you think of hell as an indescribably terrible prison, as a place of torture from which you can't escape. It can be described like that, but only figuratively—only, if you like, poetically. The poet can tell us something about his love by saying she is like a red, red rose. But we are not meant to take the description literally.

In the same way we can speak of hell as this or the other sort of place. But it isn't literally a place. It's a condition. It is what a man is like, not somewhere he is sent. It is terribly important that we should understand this, since at the back of our minds there may be a picture of God sending people to hell, as a dictator sends political opponents to a concentration camp. But it isn't a case of sending people anywhere. It's a case of what people are. Put it this way. If you take snuff, the natural result is to sneeze, and a great deal of the pleasure of snuff consists in the sneezing. On the addict, however, the snuff ceases to work in this way. He longs to sneeze, but can't. Now that is what hell is. It is desperately wanting what you have made yourself absolutely incapable of getting.

Now men and women want all sorts of things and want some of them very badly. But in the end it all boils down to one thing, and one thing only. They want to be fully alive—wonderfully, gloriously alive.

This, for instance, is the fascination of being in love. In the presence of the beloved we seem to reach a height and intensity of living normally unknown to us. Or look at the average mother with her small child. Her contented happiness is a sign that she is living on a new scale. Or consider so-and-so who has got what is for him exactly the right job. He is quite a different man. He used to be such a bore, full of self-pity. Now you feel better for meeting him. Quite a lot of what we want is really a substitute for living, or rather it consists of a sort of forlorn hope for life. Look at the advertisements we are always seeing. Dress in a certain kind of clothes, ponder over a certain kind of drink, drive a certain kind of car, and you will be as alive as the people in the picture are supposed to be. These are unimportant trifles. We're not completely taken in by the advertisement, and even if we are, we're soon disillusioned once we possess the commodity.

But there are some very much more serious kinds of fraud which promise to give us life and, in fact, reduce us to a living death. And here we are in the hinterland of hell. For example, one of the chief ways in which we are made more alive is by our personal contact with other people. But such contact, if it is to deepen and mature, requires us to respect the other as a personal individual with an outlook and needs and destiny of his own. This means that I mustn't treat him as a character in a novel I'm writing, whom I can make into what I like. He is himself. He is not what I would like him to be or think I need him to be. But the fact that he is him, and not my portrait of him, introduces an element of risk into our relation. Wouldn't it be safer to insist that, willy-nilly, he should be my version of him? And so I try to dominate him, and to possess him like a favourite picture. But this apparently pleasing prospect is a fraud. For I can never dominate and possess another person in this way. The tragedy is that I go on trying to. I can't stop myself trying to. And the more I try, the more the real him eludes me. Thus I try harder, and so I go on and on and on. That which was meant to bring me life, brings me death. I am in hell.

Or consider that job we spoke of just now, the job which was exactly right for me. I've been doing it now for twenty years, and with great success. Naturally, I've enjoyed doing it in a way; I suppose everybody enjoys doing what they do well. Yet, curiously enough, from another point of view, it's been a tremendous disappointment. I notice sometimes that I'm getting awfully bitter. I suppose this means I'm unhappy. I give my work everything I've got. I live for it. Even on holiday I'm always thinking about it, planning and so on. When I get back, my plans generally work even better than I expected. It's odd that this has ceased to give me any satisfaction. It even makes me feel angry sometimes, discontented and angry. 'Here we go again,' I think, 'and what about me, about me?' I'm the boss. I can do what I like. But when I leave the office, I shall take a lot of papers home with me and spend all the week-end working at them. It won't bring me any joy, I know that, but what else can I do? My job is everything. Without those papers, I should have nothing, so I *must* take them home. Harder and harder work, that's all I am capable of now. It's amusing to think how other men envy me.

It may be that outside the office of this business tycoon a man in the early forties is hanging about. He doesn't envy the boss; not because he knows the boss is in hell, but because business success doesn't appeal to him. His friends sometimes call him Don Juan, and he doesn't object. He's quite willing to admit he lives for women, although by this time the boast has gone rather stale. It used to give him a thrill chasing after them, a thrill of expectation. He was generally successful all right. But in these experiences he never really found what he was looking for. For all the temporary excitement, he went away unsatisfied. The only thing to do was to look out for somebody else and try again. And so he'd gone on now for years. He knew it wouldn't satisfy him, but he couldn't stop doing it. Even the temporary excitement was now wearing rather thin. It was mixed with a sort of nausea, due to his previous experience that it couldn't bring any happiness. It was as though he had become the slave of an empty ritual. He must do it, even though it had long ceased to bring him anything at all except a sense of meaninglessness.

Jesus once spoke of hell—'where their worm dieth not, and the fire is not quenched.' Scholars tell us that if you translate this and the surrounding passage back into Aramaic, the language Jesus actually spoke, you find that in form it is poetic. It has the rhythm and repetition and so forth which clearly make it poetry. In view of this, it is certain that Jesus is not here giving detailed information about the fate of the lost. He is using picture language to hint at a certain kind of inner condition—'where their worm dieth not, and the fire is not quenched.' The imagery suggests maggots and the perpetual burning of the rubbish dump. It would be hard to think of a better way of describing the state of a man who desperately wants what he has made himself incapable of getting. Desire continues to burn, ultimately the desire for abundant life, and this gives him no rest. He tries to get this abundant life from what can never give it to him. His frantic attempts, on the contrary, turn him into something no better than a corpse, on which maggots prey. And so it goes on for ever.

But is it for ever? That, after all, is the absolutely vital question when we are talking about hell. The answer is 'Yes' and 'No.'

The answer is 'Yes.' When, in ways I've tried to describe earlier in this talk, when I'm in hell there is a sort of 'for ever' quality about my experience. I try hopelessly to get life in this or that way. And although it doesn't work, I know I shall go on doing it to-morrow and to-morrow and to-morrow. I'm an addict, a spiritual alcoholic. There is no reason why I should ever stop. And if I go on living after I die, it will be the same me, the person I've made myself into, not somebody else. The same me, compelled by habit to look for freedom and life in what brings only frustration and death. Please note that it isn't a case of my being punished for ever by some external authority whose power I cannot resist, as though some schoolmaster were to send a small boy to prison for life for talking during a lesson. Hell is not a sentence imposed by an autocrat. It's me. It's what I have become by a natural and inevitable law. 'Can the Ethiopian change his skin, or the leopard his spots? then may ye also do good, that are accustomed to do evil.'

But if, from one point of view, the answer is 'Yes, it is for ever,' from another and more final point of view the answer is 'No.' In New Testament times people described their captivity to themselves by means of a mythology different from our own. They didn't speak of complexes and compulsions. They spoke of demons, principalities, and powers, who filled the atmosphere and made slaves of men. In terms of this type of thinking, I was in hell because I was the prisoner of the demons. It is therefore highly significant that in the Gospels one of the chief activities of Jesus is described as the casting out of demons. The Evangelists regarded it as powerful evidence that God's salvation had arrived—while St. Paul says of Christ that, by His death and resurrection, He disarmed the principalities and powers, stripped them of their weapons and triumphed over them. Mankind was therefore no longer their victim. Christ had set at liberty those that were bruised. Translated into our own language, this means that men can, after all, break loose from what they have made themselves into. What I have become by a natural and inevitable law is not the final edition of myself. It seems impossible when you think of the power exercised by the habits of a lifetime. And, indeed, with men it is impossible, but not with God. For Christ has harrowed hell.

How is it done? May I, at this point, remind you of what I said last week? For Christians, Christ is not only an historical figure of the past. He is the creator of the universe who Himself fills what He continuously holds in being. When, therefore, Christ changes a man, delivers him from the power of hell, He may do so by coming to him within the normal order of things, by means of circumstances. Do you remember George Eliot's Silas Marner, the miser who lived for the gold he was accumulating? The gold was stolen, leaving Silas desperate. By a chance set of circumstances a small orphan girl finds her way into his cottage. He adopts her and finds the abundant life he was always looking for. This short novel is worth reading. There is no religion in it in the technical sense, but the story is a magnificent example of how what theologians call grace works. We have no right to suppose that God ceases to work upon us when we leave this world. He doesn't change. Wherever we are, He doesn't cease to be the Saviour who delivers our soul from the nethermost hell.

Meanwhile let us remember that in some way or other we may now be in hell. If we do, perhaps we shall understand something of those circumstances of our lives which seem designed only to hurt and bruise us. For maybe in them God is seeking to woo us from long-established patterns of feeling and thinking. Maybe He is harrowing our hell too.

IV

HEAVEN

WHEN last week we were thinking of hell, we saw that it wasn't a place to which people were sent, but a condition—what they were like. The same is true of heaven. It may be necessary sometimes to describe heaven as a place, but that is because we can often speak of it only in poetic terms, or allegorically, as Bunyan spoke of the Delectable Mountains. Of course we all know this. But we are sometimes curiously blind to its implications. If heaven is what I'm like, then it can't be something I am awarded as a result of anything I do or don't do. The schoolboy is given a half-holiday as a result of having worked hard at his sums. Heaven isn't the holiday. A truer parallel would be the boy's future mathematical ability. This isn't something extraneous awarded to the boy as a prize. It's what the boy has become. If we grasp this distinction, we can dispose once and for all of a recurring controversy. Did Jesus promise rewards to His followers or did He not? If He didn't, it is claimed, His message was ultimately meaningless. It made no difference whether you responded to His call or not. If He did, on the other hand, it is claimed, He reduced goodness to having an eye to the main chance. But if heaven is what I'm like, these arguments are beside the point. I'm not rewarded as a result of being good.

My condition is itself the reward. If, for example,

I'm the sort of person who can give himself away without reserve, then there is nothing else I need or want. I am in heaven. Jesus hinted at this to His disciples when He said: 'My meat is to do the will of Him that sent Me, and to finish His work.'

We find more than a hint of it in the story of Christ's Transfiguration. He spoke, we are told, to Moses and Elijah about His coming death. His transfiguration was thus shown to reveal the true heavenly glory of what He did when He gave Himself away on Calvary. It was, as the Epistle to the Hebrews says, 'for the joy that was set before Him,' that He endured the cross—the joy of heaven.

I think that part of our difficulty in understanding what heaven is springs from a deep and hardly conscious conviction that goodness is really unrewarding. We like to feel we've done our duty, but the actual doing of it is tiresome or difficult; an uphill struggle, which brings us nothing. This in turn, I suspect, springs from a tendency most of us have to try and live beyond our spiritual income. As always, it is easier for us to see it in other people. I'm lonely and that do-gooder, Smith, has me to tea. He talks and pretends he is enjoying it immensely. But it has a terribly depressing effect on me, for it is easy enough to see below the surface. Smith is really bored. He is giving me tea, not because it is a natural expression of what he is, not because he wants to, but because he is trying to be what he isn't, because he thinks he ought to. He is living beyond his spiritual income. It therefore never occurs to him that heaven will be like giving a lonely man tea, that heaven just *is* this. How can heaven be like *his* tea-party, with its forced laughter and artificially sustained interest? Little wonder that on my way home I call at the local for a quick one. Here I meet Jones, who buttonholes me for half an hour's talk. This is refreshing. The talk is spontaneous and amusing. Jones is just being himself. He enjoys meeting new people and having a chat. And this communicates itself to me. He makes me feel worthwhile. And although, except as a joke, he won't say that his idea of heaven is having a beer with a friend, the notion wouldn't depress him. Come to think of it, he'd add, that's not too bad a parallel. You see, Jones was not trying to live beyond his income. That's why he enjoyed himself so much, and it was his natural enjoyment which did me good. Jesus once said something about keeping within one's income. 'Which of you, desiring to build a tower, does not first sit down and count the cost, whether he has enough to complete it? Otherwise, when he has laid a foundation, and is not able to finish, all who see it begin to mock him, saying, This man began to build, and was not able to finish.'

Heaven, therefore, is being what you are. 'Consider the lilies of the field, how they grow. They toil not, neither do they spin. And yet I say unto you, that even Solomon in all his glory was not arrayed like one of these.' Just be myself—like the lilies of the field—but what an absurd description of heaven. Suppose I'm the sort of person who wants to go round hitting people on the head with a hammer? Yes, I see the objection. But it all depends on how you answer the question: 'What is man?' Christians believe that God gave the answer on the first Christmas Day, that in Jesus we see man as God intends him to be, man therefore as he really is. Great or small, our deviations from the character of the Christ show that we are not yet ourselves, just as the Prodigal Son did not, as the story has it, come to himself until he realized what he was missing—'How many hired servants of my father have bread enough and to spare.' What we call our sins are attempts to find ourselves. Attempts to *be*, doomed to failure because we haven't realized what we really are. If I want to hit people on the head with a hammer, that is because I can't bear not being. At all costs I must prove to myself that I am. In fact, I don't prove it, and so I have to try again. In the last analysis, your do-gooder is in the same plight. He, too, is trying to prove to himself that he is, by his good works. And he, too, fails. For man, you see, is not his own creator. He can't make himself. 'Can any of you, for all his anxiety, add one cubit's growth to his stature?' A great deal of our goodness consists in the anxious attempt to do just this, trying to be morally and spiritually bigger men than we are. No wonder we hope that, whatever heaven is, it won't be like this.

How, then, am I to become myself? How am I to reach heaven? Am I to be like the man of Hong Kong who never did anything wrong because all day he lay on his back with his head in a sack? Am I to be passive? Of course not. But waiting, you know, is a form of activity. Let us say, I have a long and difficult letter to write arising from something which happened this morning. If I rush immediately to my desk, the words won't come. I can concoct a letter all right, but it will be a very bad one, which won't at all express my real views of the situation, so I wait until to-morrow or the next day, getting on meanwhile with my ordinary work. While I wait in this way, quite a lot of activity is going on inside me. For the time comes when I sense that I'm no longer empty of ideas, that I'm ready to write the letter. I have, of course, to make myself sit down at the desk, take paper and ink, and begin writing. But then what has been storing itself up within me comes to my assistance. The words flow freely. The letter is not concocted. It is a genuine expression of what I feel, and because of that, writing it becomes a pleasure. While I was waiting to write, the unobservant and inexperienced might have accused me of being passive. My good letter now shows how wrong they were.

Christians sometimes speak of waiting upon God. I was doing that when I waited to write my letter, even if I didn't think of it in that way. For God is not only, over against me, Somebody Else. He is also the fount of my being, the source from which I proceed. I therefore find Him within myself. And thus I cannot wait upon myself without, at the same time, waiting upon Him. He is to be found in that part of me of which I am unaware, that part of me which is working while the part of me I know is waiting. He is to be found, too, in the ordinary or extraordinary circumstances of my life. That was the great message of the old Hebrew prophets. God was there in what was happening—in the unfaithfulness of Hosea's wife, in the birth to Isaiah of a son, in the invasion of Israel by the heathen Assyrians, of which Amos said: 'Prepare to meet thy God, O Israel.' God is also to be found when we wait upon Him deliberately and consciously in prayer and worship. It is thus at sundry times and in divers manners that God makes Himself known to us. Sometimes we would naturally describe it as that. Sometimes we wouldn't. It makes no difference. He is there. And His presence is always creative. Always it is making us into what we really are. Always it is slowly enabling us to be ourselves. When you try to dominate and control the process, like the sinners and do-gooders, then you are not becoming yourself. All that this attempt to be your own creator does is just to keep you a tiny fraction of what you really are. It shuts the gate of heaven against you. This is only saying in our own idiom what St. Paul said in his when he insisted that we are justified by faith, not by works. 'So then it is not of him that willeth, nor of him that runneth, but of God that showeth mercy.'

Traditional theology tells us that heaven is the vision of God. Like all theological statements, this can be misleading as well as illuminating. For it isn't a matter of just staring; what we see makes us what we are, so that when we see God fully we shall be fully ourselves. In this state of perfect fulfilment there is no difference between rest and activity. Activity will be our rest. For it won't be a struggle to be what we aren't—that is what wears us out. Our activity will consist in being what we are, and this is the very essence of rest. I remember a preacher once saying that in heaven we shall be given new worlds to conquer, and feeling very depressed at the prospect. But I see now I was wrong. Whatever we are given to do will be peace and joy and contentment. For it will be simply us being us, like God

Himself, whose activity is simply an expression of what He is.

Please notice at this point that I'm not allowing my imagination to run riot describing some never-never land. I'm speaking of something of which we already have experience. From time to time we know what it is to be in tune, to be in the state where nothing is impeding us from being fully alive. And this, as I have said, is heaven. It comes from the temporary removal in us of the barriers which prevent us from using and articulating our full potency. This full articulation of everything we are is, in God's mercy, our inheritance. It makes us heirs; heirs of God, and joint heirs with Christ, in whom all fullness dwells. So heaven is what our human life here is about. We are on this earth in order to get to heaven, and at all times and in all places it is possible for us to arrive. And if, here and now, we are not always there, we believe that God is faithful, and that He who began a good work in us will perfect it, until we attain unto a perfect man, unto the measure of the stature of the fullness of Christ.